Other titles in the UWAP Poetry series (established 2016)

A History Of
What I'll Become

Jill Jones

Jill Jones was born in Sydney and has lived in Adelaide since 2008. She has previously published 11 full-length books of poetry and a number of chapbooks. Recent books include *Viva the Real* (UQP), shortlisted for the 2019 Prime Minister's Literary Awards for Poetry and the 2020 John Bray Poetry Award, and *Brink* (Five Islands). In 1993 she won the Mary Gilmore Award for her first book of poetry, *The Mask and the Jagged Star* (Hazard Press). *The Beautiful Anxiety* (Puncher & Wattmann) won the 2015 Victorian Premier's Literary Award for Poetry. Other works include *Broken/Open* (Salt), which was shortlisted for *The Age* Poetry Book of the Year 2005 and the 2006 Kenneth Slessor Poetry Prize, and *Screens, Jets, Heaven: New and Selected Poems* (Salt), which won the 2003 Kenneth Slessor Prize. With Michael Farrell, she co-edited *Out of the Box: Contemporary Australian Gay and Lesbian Poets* (Puncher & Wattmann). Her work is represented in a number of major anthologies, including *The Macquarie PEN Anthology of Australian Literature*, *Contemporary Australian Poetry* and *The Penguin Anthology of Australian Poetry*. An entry on her work is included in the current edition of *The Oxford Companion to Modern Poetry in English*. In late 2014 she was poet-in-residence at Stockholm University. She is co-publisher, with Alison Flett, of Little Windows Press. She is a member of the J.M. Coetzee Centre for Creative Practice, University of Adelaide, and teaches there in the Department of English and Creative Writing.

Jill Jones
A History Of
What I'll Become

Poetry

First published in 2020 by
UWA Publishing
Crawley, Western Australia 6009
www.uwap.uwa.edu.au

UWAP is an imprint of UWA Publishing,
a division of The University of Western Australia.

THE UNIVERSITY OF
WESTERN
AUSTRALIA

 A catalogue record for this
book is available from the
NATIONAL LIBRARY OF AUSTRALIA National Library of Australia

Designed by Becky Chilcott, Chil3
Typeset in Lyon Text by Lasertype
Printed by McPherson's Printing Group

 uwapublishing

MIX
Paper from
responsible sources
FSC® C001695

For Annette

'walking with daylight'

I acknowledge the Kaurna people, the traditional custodians and songmakers of the country where most of these poems were written and where this manuscript was put together, and I pay my respects to their elders, past, present and emerging. Sovereignty was never ceded.

παντοδάπαισι μεμειχμένα χροίαισιν
...glistening with so many colours
Sappho, Fr. 152

Our sweetest songs are those that tell of saddest
thought
Percy Bysshe Shelley, 'To a Skylark'

Might I but moor – Tonight –
In Thee!
Emily Dickinson, [Wild Nights] No. 269

Here's moss. How the smell of it lingers
On my cold fingers!
Katherine Mansfield, 'Sorrowing Love'

shattered in the wind
H.D., 'Sea Lily'

Any one knows that rowing is dangerous. Be alright.
Be careful. Be angry. Say what you think.
Gertrude Stein, 'Lifting Belly'

Le réel est étroit,
le possible est immense.

The real is narrow,
the possible is immense.

Alphonse de Lamartine
Œuvres complètes de Lamartine

Dans la nature
rien ne se crée,
rien ne se perd,
tout change.

In nature
nothing is created,
nothing is lost,
everything changes.

Antoine-Laurent de Lavoisier
Traité élémentaire de chimie

Contents

I was walking down the street hearing all the noise, even the quietest piece of dust. I was improvising times, positions, loves, disasters. I kept walking with dream and daylight, where I'd wake to your words in the mighty charm of the world. Breath is all I have.

My eyelashes are ways of misremembering, and the way I see each morning is more than adjustment.

No, it's more refusal, or a method of seeing that's neither straight nor shiny.

Everyone is somewhere.

Becoming Us On The Grass

if I is another then are we
                  still becoming beyond
    all this angry martial light
                    the camo effect of emojis
instead of ten thousand kisses
                        bliss floats so does shit
    and plastic but instead of
                      my silicones and polymers
my e. coli DNA trail tripping
                      on a stolen opioid scrip
    here's a field of corellas
                    white on green, could be us, love
out there on the racy grass
                    in another older light
    as if everything ancient is
                    weird queer as if renounced
forsaken by fission and the virtual
                    rather than the vertiginous
    as I fall over days, in the gritty
                    this is me, schmick, 'actual photo'
and when haven't we all been dying
                    that's still ancient while I'm standing
    in the winter parklands alive
                    as the raven who's been singing
among flights of air, of sheer now
                    of more and everything, I am
    not you but you're almost here
                    and then we will too, becoming

With Or Without Dresses

There's grace in falling apart
Above birds chase at each other
There are animals without dreams
in my dreams, they carry different ideas
no nakedness, just what they are
Claws, beaks and wings

Unlike the transparent city
never a place to hide
Its blood is everywhere
long but not eternal
neither is fucking
It will stop one day
It began somewhere once on
some ground only half forgotten
Like all the animals that grew
out of the ground
Like the crushed rose inside me
the small breeze flounce
the eucalypt flame

I dream of falling through gaps
and clutches of people dressing up
or without dresses
But potency keeps rousing
turning back to the dark
over plastic beads, blurry hems,
body funk, gravemulch
sweet weeds and moss

Where Do You Look?

The world's full of women you can't see.
They hang in the bedroom.
See the torn thread.

See what their eyes invent or ignore.
But don't look at me.

I wonder what the carpet sees
or the red ceiling.

My eyes are never the same
in the wild light indoors.

I wonder where I am in this scene
or what my hands say.
As if I know something you don't.

There's a mystery in every detail.
Even my hair is singing.

I watch a carnival emerging
from every fancy hat.

Here's what I look like in reality.
There's nothing nice
and people stare at you.

Have I told you where I got
this tiny scar? Do you see?

Each moment is an event
in the heart-breaking light.

Look directly!
It may not free either of us
but we could meet.

It's like a blind date
or a trip.

You're somebody on the street
and I go to you.

What The Glass Holds

The shape of the glass
is not the same
as what the glass holds.

The shape of the water
is infinite pleasure
inside bodies
and around them.

The shape of the glass
reminds me of the night
you first arrived.

The shape curves
in my hand.

The glass is the shape
of morning and night.

The glass reflects
the green and yellow light
from the garden
and the water there
in the air and
the ground.

The water tastes of all
and nothing, of its
internal bonds, of
where it's been.

The shape of the glass
may one day break.
Water may break.
We will too, into our
water, air and ground.
Today is every day
until then.

I drink to all that.
To what the glass holds.
And what it doesn't.

These Things (little song)

night And   it
enters me an alarm already my body
Can   I hold you   It   is difficult
being shape   Full   of whistles indirection

I'm   not prepared panic   is no excuse
an ambulance   as avenues Pass I   am
passing as a human With   as much skin They
attach a monitor I   remember that.

Perhaps   I could be   a beach Or   part of
an ocean Perhaps   yes that siren Perhaps   no

I daydream   at night And   read old stories
of   a coach That   arrives for me   at last
in this   wintry dark   a   life form
dirty   as   everything

Re. Composure

Peel me some language
taste my reflection
stretch my skin with it
stone my composure.

Swivel my orange
expose my meticulousness
crawl through my electricity
flick my bloody awareness.

Somersault my disturbance
comfort me with amnesia
love my LED at midnight
recompose me.

Defraud my surplus
defray my averages.
Junk me junk me junk me
with possibility.

Test my day with an iron
rejig my fortunes.

Oh Venus, That Zenith

In the morning media rustle
we look for our vertebrae
    our balance, anything sensible
      shoes or daycream
encase our nipples although
    we fancy being free
as the train gushes and swallows
    tickets and selfies, hi-vis
      and daydream

Then the city's coarse daylight
opens its cracks
    the paving jerk, escalator drag
      a last gulp
so our mouths might swell
    with sexual tannins
      a cafe's smoke tongue
before swipe and thrust

Goodbye cruel air, you weepy green trees
    crushed yellow light
The lift slackens to the tenth floor
We remember nothing now
apart from the gash in night
    good ol' dog Sleep
running about under red moon
    and white cliffs and how
      we fall there, and there

Oh Venus I don't forget you
   in the spread
of tinted morning, the grids
I've wandered far in circles
   around your heights
without shoes or sensibilities
      I don't forget you
and how I've climbed
into another balance, cusp
   flexure, fold
another arc and then
another

Walking Home In The Dark Through A Succession Of Categories

I hold the keys tight in my hand, I hold
the night close and distant, I hold my thoughts
close to my disquiet, I hold my tightness like
a resistance, I'm not trespassing in the world, this
path is my own breath – shadows are grainy thoughts,
tricksters, surfaces, they begin stalking, and above,
wires float in ancient rage reborn, the newest gust
broadcasting nonstop desiring and despising, unlike
these trees, these fecundities, shelters, sighs, whose
forms under stars hold birds – I try to ignore
the cybernated howl mocking this body me, this body
my claim on the real along any road as though I
violate it, that howl of beastly excuse for
despoiling – shadows begin talking as they fleet and ghost
as though darkness is nothing though it is fully
here – dark is a contour, a fabric, a curtain, a cover,
in the way dark extends itself, I breathe it in, something
cruel or casual, something kind, can I also be something
of the dark hiding – I hold myself, this body a surface,
a well, I hold this scapula, rib, patella, I call to myself,
whispering through the throat's isthmus, I advise
all my bones, 'you hold', I advise my nerves, 'you hold',
my blood 'stay quiet, within', if I breathe out a cry,
am I more real – I hold myself close, as if holding
is anxiety and strength, as if I am shadow,
suggestion, memory, a house of spirits, I hold
my place and my fear, as primal in the way bellies are
for birth and the fist, what shows up on my skin are
other truths – if I eat words, do I swallow lies, whose

language breath will I exist in tonight, if not the owl
or the breeze, a language that is trickster, cover,
lie, suggestion, a howl, a murmur – I am not
a story to tell, I am not someone's metaphor, the dark
isn't a symbol, it's a time when I walk – there are no
memorials and no armistice, as though everybody
forgets, this woman that woman, darkness is pierced
as it pierces – my feet crunch over the season, falling
is a perpetual season, leaves fall, my voice falls into
myself, if I meet another voice, another
hand, another truth – if I fall in the dark, who
will hear

This Path Is Our Season Tonight

Lone or in love, I've cursed much. Still,
Androgynous dusk.   my lips work, the hankering
Its flickery shadow   spoken. Flowers explode.
pathway among bat squeak.   Even if we fall away
Argumentative dark.   past the gates. Still, you're
A swooping conversation.   here, crazy here.
Whisper cell light into your hand, starlight.
A hum half-woken.   Even if sky demands dark.
Walk and joke past pine   Yes, I await you even
and oak. Flowers exhale   in storms. Shall we kiss
when they bloom and   in rickety bliss? O queer night
explode once more.   warm us, keep us in keeping.
Up in the galaxy sea, stars reform. More than
Haze rewrites other couples   thought is born.
human waft, pink half-light.   Our cloudy mouths
Blackbird and cicada sing   breezing attitude. Then
with a stray dog, and   clarity clears our tongues.
our bent season.   Midnight shakes out its angels.

One City Is Another (space mix)

One city is another city   I clothe   streets
                                pluck   luxury
  One city is green and blue   each word   a stitch
                            one city   and yellow
arpeggios seams heels dreams   it all goes   around (and around)
                            the cadence   adjusts
  each city late at night

                     I dress like the moon
                         that meddle
I dress like the sun   arrogant   teasing
                    I fumble with chambers
  I play all the organs   I failed   the room
                   I repeal   blush
There are roads throughout   needless
                   figments (figments figments)

  I was born in the afternoon   chafe at fashion fuss
      fragments   in my homely head

Improvising: What I'll Become

I am assembled
a history of what I'll become

Far off there are holdfasts
cosmos winks, metal and darkness

The mind is also a swirl
needless opera

The divine numbers are a gamble
zero is a place to begin

Trees invent shadow

I cope with presence
a baffling besotted twilight
I sweep dust out the door

There is no pause button
in this immodest heat

I wake up in fragments
a prayer that never surfaces

I bless every idea, glance and jot

The Doll And Me

I hate the doll, its plumpy head,
its brunette swirls, its itsy cheeks,
its pout, its lashes, the uptight clothes,
marrowless arms, nerveless teeth,
its squeaking, the mess
it makes on the floor.
I want to detach the twee wee feet
and hammer it to the fence, drown it,
skewer it to the door, to say 'this is what
has become of us'. Even naked
it makes me angry and afraid.

What if the doll grows? What if
it wants to take me home?
What if the doll ships are waiting,
doll planes, neverending
pink clouds and puffy oceans?
What if the doll says 'I could begin
to take you apart', and
pins a dress to my hollows,
paints me so I smile
at every beastly, devouring kiss?

No, no, no! I must throw it into
the ecstatic sky. Hook it to a comet.
Just like all the monsters
in their filthy skirts, who says
it can't crash and burn in
rapt and stupefying bliss?

Cursing Girl Gust

o what! spare us   heroes & *heofen*
though I look like   the almost-you
there is other craft   rare & raw
in my wit's hoard

I have no show-brag   trick kiss
my uncomely   dross-dress
plain-face hide   & hunch-mind
my down-dark   leant in cunning

fuck you fey-fickle foe   pest-face
you'll not play in the   cut of me
don't sweet-wif me   wanker
you sack-head creep   between walls

what am I   your nemesis
yr woe & yr drag   yr big fall
so you shall   to yr dust-world
no-heaven   I'll do the cut of you

I was tough-wrought   ain't wreck yet
but so long you   so heck you
I'm cloud-friend   & storm-born
the not-this not-that   you bet yr other

Patience Without Virtue

Everyone loves the female voice.
Am I forgiven for having one?
I wait patiently, hoping it's only
to do with simple flowers. It never is.

I dissent again, the moon goes as it came.
There's nothing transcendental within reach.
What must I do amongst sweat
grey flannel, car parks, and theories?

I can only be a certain kind of lunatic
and women are vaster than history.
It's the way I don't step forward politely.
No point sitting on the fence.

It's the way I have to fix things
by painting a sign. 'I can't believe
I still have to protest this fucking shit.'
I can't put the leaves back.

My affinity is always a question.
I can't recall when these things didn't happen
in my cells or beaten-up memories.
I'll never be as dead as a man.

Mouth Form Flower

Let fault flaw
Let the fence fall
Let's flabbergast the goal with tongues
Let debacle warp in dawn
Let beginning bury end
Let a hundred pods blush

Let the mouth form flower
Let flesh flash
Let's lick plethora
Let erosion jabber in the gown
Let's find fit and make do
Let's sieve without shock

Let debris fill rust
Let myriad dapple and draw
Let's spurn our quote marks
Let's trick death perception
Let limit out
Let not mere quintessentials

Let wreckless wreck more
Let cloth drop
Let's lay waste the hours

Let's not say

Let a thousand errors bloom

This Crumbling Aura

There's nothing sacred about me. I was born under stars
that kept moving. Outside I could smell lost temperatures
stolen dust   my blood tainted with history.
But here I am without a prayer   looking for gods in everything
that's melting. I watch the littlest sparrow. It knows
where the crumbs are.

I broke marriage. I never fitted shoes. And where would I walk?
In the dark men will kill you   and in scuzzy city light as well.
I'm never better than in some unknown country
called a dream   though even there men kill me.

And even here I wake up in my own breath, the only thing
I've given back, scuzzy, scared   tainted   nothing holy
even in the way I walk past seats and palms   where girls
look like Debbie Harry or Chrissie Amphlett   in songs out of
another time, a virtual place   my local understanding
shimmering along my skin   as an iffy aura, a rapture, pleasure
and pain.

All I am is a jump cut, montage   a fiction to myself
in my profane air, badly edited   but knowing where the crumbs are.
I'm inhabited by stories, fevers, voices and lies   heaving
this breathing into light that changes every moment. There's no way
to rescue me, even as a translation of an original hymn.
Am I simply my little secret?

Sometimes the dark is just the way a room is
or that part of a blink   that flicker of closing.

Everyday Phantasms

the music of the kitchen
is like a stranger's lament

the fridge coughs and swears
as if it had another story to tell

something it would only confess
to someone it will never meet again

*

time is the arranger
all things bend in it

dust is everything's memorial

*

a pale orange glow
shines on the road out of town

*

I lean beyond the line
and shimmer

*

somewhere the dark's spirits
are regained
the spirits that are never named

who's the visitor
the grass, or me

*

why is everyone so afraid of thinking
even the walls look sceptical

*

magpie lands on the rail next to me
balances, excretes quickly, then chases
just visible scraps on the table

one tiny tomato-red item
is the last to go down

*

outside ideas
are other ideas

the air jostles with
every particle of wish thought

*

how dreams perform
my alternative life

how these hours form
in a stream of phantasms
in late rooms and air

*

a white man with a NWA cap

a table of scones and cream
alcohol wipes, sugary tea

weather-beaten women
stories in the creases

an old Shania Twain song

*

do you believe in your own sentience

to evolve in the ground
even that is not final

*

a McDonald's sign, the snaking freeway
polluted dusk
its black vegetation

*

in the parklands trees are waiting
as if they knew all along

*

if I am found dead on the bus
do not blame the bus

if I am found alive
thank the bus for getting me away

if I am found
was I lost at some older hour

Almost

I had guilt, not enlightenment,
and it was tight as ironing.
I had curiosity in curlers, bouffant outrage
a childhood's bitterness with tomato sauce
a dip of Dad's alcohol
when nothing made sense at all.

I almost felt like a man when I knew something.
Or a woman when I knew I had a secret to keep.
It's one way of forming an attitude, along with
wonder or dread.

Is celery boring? Does it matter? I remember
that fried ice-cream wasn't, it was
something like blue eye shadow, flowery ties
bouncy melancholy and a lot of guitars.
Almost as good as real spaghetti, or fish and chips.
In fact, so much better for once.

Sometimes I think I'm really a list,
a grocery list, a total of outlandish positions,
or impossible recipes. Mostly that.
Or a poem on a home-made card someone keeps
and forgets. Sitting in a box. Dangerous.
Lost. Unsaid. Guilt again.

About my voracious mouth. This daughter tongue.
A woman. At a table. Tasting
a name on my skin.

Consummations

the spinning world
     the guttural dark
sounds the skin   & leaves you
     a book of consummations
fresh as rot & queer within

*

in the torn fabric
     the ancient salvage
it's all moving
     clues   charms   throngs
the dearest ground

*

exhale
     between breath bones
no moment more free
     horizon   potent
enough to be touched

There were times within the city that bodies could not only die but could also be free in the way streets don't always recognise you. I never planned to be more than a day ghost.

There were times I dressed so tight the blood disappeared. I then became all nerve. Dressing hurt as much as bruises and wheezes. But how can I ignore all my naked.

There were times the city allowed our bodies to wander on wide streets, dancing as if it would be alright, as if parading or loosening the bonds of lace or chains was somehow liberation.

City Of The Interior

And you're always for me   even in days of gall
and days of gusto, of sore   of slump, of sheen
of kisses that never end   or barely arrive
of days approaching the last days   or the first day
in the city of pranks, the city   of hullabaloo
the city of amorous   and ambiguous ploys, the city
where diamonds hide   in our pockets like lost toys
the way air clasps at   the dexterity of fences and sharp
glassy markets   where I guess rather than figure on
the paper skin that carries the shimmer   of my ardent vote.

And here I have written   the number one
though the number of   your hands is always two
that's two for my face   then two for my waist
then two for the vestige   of such a one on a street
only you'd see, the one   who prowls ever softly
among the white, purple   and cloudy paths and maybe
becomes tangible like tinnitus   or aliens broadcasting
arrivals in the breast   of the world, the bright clump
the brave corner   a vision of canticles amongst
debris, the city of   last women standing, or
a small town of crystalline rain   that gusts as it comes.

And what if I told you   there are no safe bets
only slipping of skin into   a city of ample interiors
canticles and clasping, of brio   and what hands say
at every ambiguous breast   in the city of lost ideas
lost hearts gathering   voluptuous envoys
at the hush end of the street.

Where We Go

C'mon, let's go with our attention depending,
with the ardour of late afternoon's pink horizon,
its cloud tendril, bird scrawl, and our questing
attachments – 'there is such beauty' – but
it's the 'such' that contains a caution about
our exhausted hair or souls or the still sanguine way
we negotiate September's impatient buds
along the terraces, and our way through another discussion
at a corner, all the busy figures with swathed loads
and tenacity, what choices – a stop/go giggle
or something serious about the quickening splendour
of the road, its corrugations shining, a place indeed
for a hungry soul, or at least destiny full of flare,
where wires hover, machines quiver as if they know
who really owned all of this here, it's not for you and I,
not even the late shit rolling across the path, plastic
shit with purpose – there was a cost, we missed it –
the tentacles of the program spiral from the mall,
from the phones, 'it all seems so smooth', you say,
and what can I reply, what can I gesture at that's not
the same lie as memory, that's now in the program, you say
'see, even the dresses watch us, demand something from
our bodies' but I don't follow your eyes there, I take your hand,
'c'mon', I want to say, we can hitch onto a vision
outside the city's halls, past the parks, the river curves,
past the future to somewhere a bit like this as if it's actually
intense, routine and baffling like that place where we go everyday.
C'mon, let's find such beauty among our bodies
and common splendour.

Out Among Trees

Do we struggle in the room
or go out among trees?

Go a-gogo like dancing through doors
into a massive hiss, the restless demand

Our abandon on the traffic island
wavelike as the day's slickness masses

As blossom dissolves darkness
under outrageous and humid caress

Sweeping in restless make-up
smudge it here, then lavish me there

Lipstick as borrowed loveliness
if you hold the colour to your lower lip, yes

Where expression becomes miraculous
though the outside hubbubs all night long

Hold my hand as we dance, liquid and cunning
because the ends are endless

Who lights up light it's how we
dissolve through the mossy abyss

We clothe the streets, we're clothed in them
dressed like the moon, dressed like the sun

Using our bodies we scribe things on each
these symbols in our runic flesh

We go down past endless city strands
through chaos as hissy expression

Instead of struggling in a room with demands
come out among trees and wastelands all

a-gogo at once, massive, strong, reckless
all   night   long

I kiss you like restless blossom
a clasp beyond fell sickness, in ever struggle

wastelandagago   mossydarkness
restlessabyss   everstruggle

Something Wild And Multiple

The way you dissolve feelings
or into feelings like a tablet

something palatable and sweet
something pulpish

as you recite existence
even in nonexistence

it ripples your skin

its small dark happy

shaking like leaves on
a roof well-lit with tears

a light pool

a plurality

as if to get on with it
companionable with hands

to give away sex not
lose it but put it out all over

there!

huge grins or small and serious
or frightening like a storm

or an animal hunting
something wild and multiple

like time or memory's
voice coming from your head

silver bones and perils
flower in the blood

The Morning, Not The Movie

There was a time I cherished
my non-sequiturs
spent more time out of my head
in half-baked theorising
or a vagrant continuity glitch
and some gawky comeuppance

like, the sex-drugs billets-doux
of a simple girls'-night-out
that transience, routine backdrops
tracks up and down stairs
a corridor corpse and a bare-arsed man
in the courtyard, bawling

I've never enjoyed
waiting for people to do drugs
there was just enough chundering
even with my chaotic heartbeat
my pulsating deep-strange entity

like, you put yourself into
the post-punk river of traffic
or hug escalators with some
heavily ruffled drag performer
after another schooey of New
it's just the beginning
of the set-up
of alien friend technology
and the drama hug

call me sensation-seeker, in and out of
and afterwards on Bondi bleary
crammed early with desolate drams
or the garish argue
and sand squeaks in the cold

spare me the movie star looks
I defy that and horizons
before that, there's a lot of chumps
to be juggled, scroungers, pushers
liars, twerps, the proverbial
and her lips feeling weird
your friend's sister
in the unforgiving forest of light

'some lifestyle choices', says
the addict with answers
and that girl over-acting
in tights reading crime fiction
like, it was situationist slapstick
under a Henson image in
someone's mother's apartment
where among the sounds
of electronic bleeps it's getting
gritty across the surfaces

it's too early to muse on what
it is to die in this alarmed
and affronted spring
of ageing activist cameos
and expensive graffiti art-spray

in each sequence we walk away
night to morning where
there are no tunes just waves
and a pat-pat hug-hug
instead of 2am strife
to pay for our confession, and the go

(whoever dies with their speech uninjured
must live on in a special time capsule)

don't go gushing
and don't go

allow me another version
of the 'fuck you' song
and I'll try a little tenderness

Filthy Distance

It wasn't anywhere I lived
exactly, it was more like time
full of laser dust, celebrity footballers
a space of affable ravage
of being blinded afterwards.
You were always looking for surfaces
even as small as a credit card
and all this accompanied by plainsong
beaten at angles through drum machines
and consequences. Light rose
like seraphim, which seems a lazy way
to put it now at this filthy distance.
The nights preferred their ruck and maul
with averages in drinks, sex in the broom closet
ancient fairies hot with farragoes
and heels on concrete.
What can this old town do
apart from suffer when we'd turn inward
on our germs and genius
or learned to measure things in parallel.
Let's make sure the terms are clear
at least in a monetary sense. You can dance
down the field in rugger bugger kit
even now no-one thinks it queer
unless you kiss.
My tongue was bitter and the gain did not last
the fractals on the wall looked great
but they weren't the only
theory you brought me.

A View Of Elizabeth Bay House

I could have written about lost friendship
the always disappearing, you did not need
so much money then to live here, so we watched
the harbour, looked down on Boomerang from
Billyard Avenue, looked up here, sometimes, then
friendship faded, things you misunderstood
and I made those Sydney moves into the west
kept moving, collecting memory and seeing its
display in the returns you make on a sunny day
which catches on all the old built things
curves of coming and going, what harbour air
touches and changes as waters rise and all
the sounds of bells decay and you are part
of the remain as you fade before a house.

All That Shudder

That year, I went back to the city alone, me and all my noisy solitude. Everyone's now gone. I remember the way we'd gossip stories into night, along those roads, Glebe Point Road, Darlinghurst Road. Or walk to the harbour, listen to the wharves, what's left of them. Or get wasted in a loud pub to the south, towards Botany, where the planes almost drown.

Or I'm back at that corner where she said I should accept things as they are, rather than holding out something to be filled. But the glass has passed. I hear it smash to the gutter.

I remember helping another girl throw up, just here, in another century after a night nearby with booming walls, of all that survival in tune with a kiss, names and numbers on drink coasters, promises as opposed to meanings, too many women not watching you. So there I was, being gentle with this kid retching, as hellhounds scoured her insides. Night allows this tact and touch. Then she walked off. They always do.

I'm here again, listening as night's sirens shift away. Like a reprieve, like an unprepared morning. There's nothing butch in the sound of dawn, lost harmonies, or sleep.

this makebelieve this driftwood

this abundance this consumptive force begging the future
this driftwood breaking apart arguments harmonies limbo
this window this plastic viscera amps in the shadows

composing this makebelieve in paragraphs memorising privilege
sand the car sales yard this homecoming orchestra staggering in
cupboards this record jacket dirty open-weave curtains

this background signal phantom washes a broken cup
black with insects knowing this nakedness this chameleon self
spray painting manifestoes 'all doors lead to busy rooms'

gathering happy blues hyperventilating eternal focus restructuring
open-ness bottles of Johnny Walker towers of toilet paper
this cardboard the dog next-door looking through salvage

this flavouring grottoes of biscuits the sound of breaking glass
this earthen darkness anticipating rituals the back room
ask for French 'it's getting too hard' 'no' and 'yes' this mask

brown haze sweeping backwards weather memorising dust
wine and smorgasbord piano accordion classics this stuff
into thousands of pillows pulling apart in shapes of animals

Packing For The Journey

You take plastic stars, a bicycle,
a dozen pot plants, a padlock, a pencil,
enough beer, money for the ferry.
Even when you get there, or if you don't,
you take a succession of songs.
They don't have to be old as cafe songs,
they could be new as rain.
You listen as you haul, it will work out.
You see the ferry stalling on the other side
as the lights begin to come on past the quay.
You gather the things around you.
The plants need sun but here's the rain,
the plastic stars are all they have.
And the pencil, don't forget the pencil,
it draws earth below water and imagines the sun
in the starry night the ferry brings.
And you bring your things to the landing,
the gates are opening, the padlock drops away.
Even the rats in the storehouses, the fish
in the sluices, the trams on the bridges, the camp
of the homeless under the pylons, even the strays
are quiet. Except for the rain, and the engines
which begin stuttering. At least
you have the beer.
And there's enough for everyone.

Norra Hammarbyhamnen

Laundromat Near The Corner Of Passage Alexandrine

Here's to centuries of laundromats
and cigarettes, boundless fluorescence
and the coin slot, time and heat, clean towels
for all, the warmth of euros as they descend,
detergent named for animals or angels.
It's minus one, it's six o'clock and the moon
is already busy. Here, everything folds
after it spins, according to the politesse
of strangers. The room is full of greetings,
water runs all over our clothes as though
it had always meant to do so.

It's time to turn and let the colours be,
they will never stay sharp, not even
in moonlight, as fibres fray and fall till
they can no further. This is no longer
important, although we have nowhere
to go that's changed from this morning.
It was sunnier then, of course, but
what metamorphosis could we accept
so late in the moment when we have
nowhere else to go in our centuries,
our waters, or our winters that are shiny
in each uncertainty.

Improvising: Full Of Indirection

I wake up this morning
reinventing myself
from the thick weave of branches

I wasn't expecting a carnival
this perplexing delirious eclipse

I'm naked
or in someone else's clothes
full of indirection
unkempt endless thirst

I'm less articulate than grass
passing as a human
dreaming the immortal body
a large god of dust

I still smell it in my dreams
a name I'm not sure of
the hey-ho of unmooring

Dissolve And Razzle

Rat bones black and white
feather grey stones
sound of a kiss
in a car cold weather
alive with tidings
and intercourse of
throttles whistles shrikes
highway meshes and
huge belly moons low
in north-east
razzle of high heels
and lips across
the steering wheel meteors
soon and a humming
at the crest this night
as the horn of the rat's claw
will disappear into mash
earth or pick-up deposit
re-uttered from first touch
to star haze making
sounds for fallen climaxes
keys and little wonders
of this brightness night
coming into its sounds
coming in from hours
interstellar heart
of things dissolving rain

In Finite Body

To pick. To flush. To pass. To swallow.
To place. To ground. To fix. To catch.
To make. To land. To prompt. To know.
To cherish. To discount. To trim. To cover.
To concentrate. To return. To reveal. To show.
To ignore. To coalesce. To walk. To match.

To reject. To surface. To construct. To shadow.
To feel. To create. To illustrate. To work.
To amplify. To extract. To annul. To sorrow.
To affirm. To atone. To avoid. To reorient.
To attest. To occupy. To pulsate. To go.
To transcribe. To elicit. To dissolve. To see.

To sustain. To weaken. To lay claim. To follow.
To rattle. To take. To mollify. To disappear.
To run up. To pet. To value. To allow.
To stare at. To ensure. To catch. To arise.
To relax. To stretch. To pass. To grow.
To lie. To tell. To loosen. To trace

your body/ to its nouns/ to
body/real theory/ of

As Long As You Need / Fragments

As if a cute-voiced girl
in the slack limbs of eros
sweet and bitter
I still shudder.

They say don't disturb
all that washed-up trash.
Now the sea's sour as death
do I still miss all that...darlin'?

Remember our burlesque hearts
and heads relaxing on sweaty breasts
in Sydney's sun ecstasy
in its dusk-pink twinky hours.

Remember making our way
among shadowy electro-shapes
no party too hot...no dance
where we were absent.

In an old century! Of course
we did such flash young things
such wasted perfect time
such girls all those nights up long.

My mind now cracks up
as the world's fucked.
Pink and purple blossoms
rot on the footpath.

If this is my shame or pride
I must speak for what
the future will recall...even
my own disturbing junk heap.

Still...to the ends of the earth
Desires! all of them older
all of them younger all now
still lifting above the roof.

...in fabulous style...just like
honey...for as long
as you need...with these
two arms...

Abandon Careen Dawdle Blunder

You ask 'what changed everything?'
Machines, being, trade, quintessence?
Is there 'something that can save us' apart from
deep pure agitation, factories, seagulls, manacles?

'Why would you attack vagueness,
isn't this realistic?' rather than well-mannered
smeary truths, the unaccountable held in tongues,
in the blunder and careen?

In each water drop, is the rush
the coming of time, its rotting steps?
If you see everything, you see nothing.
Instead, kiss me!

'What adds up?' Rafters, windows, clover leaf
roads, lost cargo, sand on bitumen, spritz of sunlight
on your hair, working in sawdust, a courthouse,
our private nocturnes, indecorous as poems.

See that intense golden line across the bridge,
like a carving of a leaf or nest, not about itself.
Hallucinations are a kind of abandonment within
silence where old nature is still, or not so still.

'What adds up', what emptied senses? Another
speech in a media bubble. 'What's going on?' Living
on the gulf, smoke, a rising sea, the mongrel question
telling time, the gnomon, an accord, a statute.

Here's to transparency, cell renewal, flowers
in the gutter, the lines of your hands, stones
through water, dawdling en route. To be
with skin. Yes, kiss me!

In The Hour Of Glass

In almost-sung summer, along street sweat,
                              miasma-jangle
there's an odour from soft places
                              armpits of buildings
the city groin. I walk across ambiguous lines
                              at my usual angle.
I've looked to the breeze, where it was
                              last night, traces
of a flute that's returned, the vernal breath
                              drum clouds
a moon-shaved spread, as each garden
                              waves up windows.
I've laid out my eyes under cover, a lamplit
                              black shroud
air knocks on another dawn story, love's
                              unnamed country
now at sultry corners, I allay my breath of
                              a second's water
urgent, that crow calls home, after rain
                              greener than ordinary.
My minerals draw away, drip from me
                              precious metals
sucked into cloth, each drop has no end
                              the surge that passes
each door, last night's spit and perfume
                              smells invisible.
Everything is suspension, at my breaching
                              the glass.

One City Is Another (dream radio remix)

I was born in the afternoon
I wake up in fragments
in my homely forehead

I still chafe at fashion

I dress like the sun
arrogantly and teasingly
even in embrace

I fumble with chambers

I dress like the moon
around that satin breeze
Dreams are a meddle

Inside me a cadence seams

One city is green and blue
each word is a stitch
One city is another city

I am clothed in all of them

Sun Haunting

shadows and flesh seem almost at one
                 as we blink at traffic lights
late afternoon air billows with brilliance
    heat strafes our flesh, we wait here
for a signal, a reprieve, as the planet moves air
               through shifty temperatures
   we drain away, or do we, perhaps the weight
of summer is enough in west-facing journeys
   as light floods everyone's eyes
our figures wander cosmic gravities
         gusts between structures play us, taunt us
         with larger measures
sweat-tired, machine-halted, hoping
   we could blur ourselves, let sun shroud our
             bodies among buildings
    they don't see our hands touch, we skirt footpaths
        our skirts murmur between haunting the heat
our own and the city's treasury of breath

then you and I, and you and I
        repeat differently into night, damp realignments
where weather finds us draped like leaves
   together we make a foreign shape
             vagrant, deflected, beautiful
we're impossible birds, but after, in quiet
           we're truly allowed
   take me to you, in our skin's manner of radiance
     to be as new as what we carry
that's not our traces but finally rain

A Midsummer Dream

I'm wishing the continent
would drift south
for the summer
    forgetting the drama of dust

Let's forecast
more social avenues, full
of leaves, stolen diaries
brazen tags, jerking phones

For now my mouth's
too complex to kiss
and my body's arid without you

Can't we go home
without our objections
and lie down besotted
in snow at the place
where the continents
broke up
all those years ago
Let's make it up
with earth with skin

Go on, defrost me
on those old rocks
then let's go to town
knock back by a fire
cellars of Antarctic wine

And then, there we were, in another place where more airy domains were growing and space was full of leaves, things that needed tending, the tender I am not sure I'm truly capable of.

Dreams are never careful. Nor are they even possible in daylight, waking within nonchalant light. Or I'm lying, and all of corporeal life is also a dream whose language is beyond.

Somewhere something is always laughing without harm, without solace, with grace.

Nothing is permanent.

Far As The Night

'one must walk as far as the night'
without shoes yet firm to the ground
that night when the north wind rises
further than where you may be found

taking up taste of skin memory
as galaxies shift past each thought
as far as the night into bird dawn

without eyes yet bright as a star
without hope yet like a laughing clown
every coin for the hollow filling up quick
every play just one more of the game

I'll walk so far without possession
no night, no star, no skin, no ground
simply a voice, its unkempt endless thirst

The Prevailing

I wake up this morning
reinventing myself
in my eyelashes.
Outside the window
a hundred flowers bloom.
I've never seen them before.
I find one hundred
names for every one of them.

I wake up tomorrow.
There are one hundred more.
It's been like this
since I was born.
As though I'd forgotten
them or myself.

One night they'll all die.
Their names will live on.
I'll say those names
wherever there is
of echo or eternity
a strong prevailing breeze.

And I can blink my eyes
open once more.

Door

For you at the door
with a mouth full of sun
with mortal blue photos
with hazards as fictions
your hands red with plums

For you as you wait
with speckle and rainstorm
with hands rich in weather
with apricot and feather
out of garden you come

With purple and petal
as blood and appearance
for with and for when
as fabric and answer

I wake as you come
you open this one

Dream Home

I sometimes dream of always dreaming.
I don't think of that as death. But when will I wake?
When will I turn to you, go to you, come to you,
carrying night with me, the things I can't tell?
    (As if it's loss that remains, that no tongue
    can assemble within daylight.)
Maybe this dreaming is the immortal body,
dormant except in sleep, a kind of bliss that evaporates
each day, a kind of dread that escapes the waking
of shape and sinew.
    (If you die in a dream, do you? If you die
    in a dream, can you?)

A dream is a vagrant. If I wake, am I still vagrant?
Is there anything I can take with me apart from a dream?
    (Is the dream a separate country, a world I can't see?
    If I call out in a dream, who hears?)
Something shouts, something drops.
Maybe it's a dream next to my ears. Or the blind
is banging in the wind from the south.
    (It's something falling from my hand, something precious
    while I'm naked, or in someone else's clothes.)

Night isn't the length of a dream.
    (Who do I reach for in the night?)

To wake is not the opposite of dreaming.
To dream is to be unowned by anything but the dream.

The Hour Of My Death Is Always The Same

I'm cold as a moon.
I wonder how black the black earth
truly is. I can feign no more,
in this perplexing delirious eclipse,
as the sky reaches for my forehead gently,
through the impure window,
a final mark of equality.

The great sarcophagus
of the world opens.
At first it looks like a trick,
like all the things they hid – the jealousy
of skin and schooling,
how paper grates as you write,
what kissing means, why backs turn.

I see the chequered floor
and all the steps I missed.

I wasn't expecting a carnival
or some stopless dazzle, yet
there's something sumptuous in
this gossamer, this glimmer.
As if it's morning outside
where cobwebs in branches balance
the dew. Or something like
a dream.

The window faces south,
the great cold ocean.
Outside birds curse. What they've gained
or lost I still can't see, and now
I've lost them, like cars, sex,
cash, or songs.
What is distance now?

Without sinew
everything spools away,
microbes, gut coils, the body-blue jam.
You all smell like the living,
skin-covered, bright with fur
and mortal keepsakes.
You still breathe your satins and blushes,
your antidotes, thumbs, relief.

Already I'm missing
what I miss.
I miss most
that world's dirty air.

Into Our Thin Rivers

My father dies in the night
That afternoon he said to us 'get me out of here'
I know this is what the doctors have done
It's called pain killing
The next day we go to see him
His face is colder than I'd ever imagined

My mother dies at an hour I'm not told
It took less than a year
She floated on a general anaesthetic
up a river I'd never heard of
into a small room
where at the end she could say nothing

As a child I remember them covering my face
and the ticking machine that was also a river
a dark delta land full of birds
I remember its ether breath
I sometimes still smell it in my dreams
I wonder who decides to turn it off

Homeless Home

Even when the mind
   is homeless
the world is there   real and difficult

We can't understand
all we touch   but we must talk
about it

The bird I just buried   had a home
I'm not giving it a home
   or rest
Its feathers and bones   part severally

Here's one category for such a bird
   Grallina cyanoleuca
One of the ways we know
   what we don't know

Or writing it down is another

'I buried the peewee
so desiccated I couldn't tell
   its age or sex.
One of its wings   had parted
from the rest.'

The soil is so much drier
   this year
These things
   irrevocable
   fantastical   perilous

Where we're going
we don't understand
   but we know   this happens

when they bury me   burn me
finally   homeless
   home
(if there's a small garden
   of feathers
a large god of dust)

In This Season Of Emptiness

Birds flood into the city.
    They know what to do with trees
        and the high places

the never-ending lights
    the flags pigeons crap on
        (yes, those shitty shrouds).

They land on lonely statues
    in fake parks, empty

        under flat grey rain.

Cloudheads look thick on the hills
    ashen as bomb plumage

        or bushfire.

Life goes on in carparks
    toilet blocks
        drains, malls, the food courts.

Crows gather on a crane.

    They scoop what I leave.
    What does that make them (inside them)
what tangled process?

I want to drink this can of iced tea
like wine   slowly   remembering
     what anything tasted like

the first time or any time
     the glue on a stamp, blood from a cut
          honey, milk, the sea, an apple
your skin.

Something I smell
     eucalyptus, fire

          and here's the match.

If I thought shaving my head would work...

where's the razor, where's the shawl?

*

If I could   I would

leave by   the great corridor

head north

my empty   red head

aflame.

The Lost Child

The Heart

As if I'm a miniature vessel, clasping my womb, or my cup
filled with warm tea. Do I look like something
you'd find near a grave, or near a wall where men decide
who'll be sold? Or am I simply a thing, like the hair
on my head, light in morning? Although I'm clearly
visible, I'm not. Nobody knows my name. Although
my breasts are stressed, my heart is tough enough, held
together by sticky plaster.

The Gods

As if my face was made of marble, given an ancient
name etched with gold, so I'd look gradual, almost
serene, almost still, except for tiny motes
of museum dust that land on me. If that's what
being a kept woman is. There's a lost child somewhere
in the galleries, crying. It's not mine. Only the gods
know these things. (It's why death is
bad. The gods don't do it.) But, let's break
the gods, sweep out the dust, the ichor, the stain.
Let's send it all back into air. Load it all onto comets
out there in the great galaxies. Return tickets, everyone!
Let's go there just to see!

Names

I had a book about astronomy when I was a kid, *The How
and Why Wonder Book of Stars*. It was mainly pictures:
all those skies, all those unfolding heavens, shapely
planets, striped and whirling. I'll never give my name
to a star. Just as well. My name's too short for anything much.
Don't call the lost child after me. You can't make new life
by tacking together old body parts. We know where that leads,
adrift on the ice. We know the ice is melting. The lost child
wants its mother. My cup is now cold.

Fate

There's nothing heavenly around here. If they open up
my grave they'll not find me yet. Perhaps I've escaped.
The plaster in my chest itches. I don't know what
my name means. Besides, the time I arrived is not
much different to the time I'll leave. Embryos come,
embryos go, all squeezed up into sacs or wombs or
graves. Behold, the goddess of fate is standing with me.
Who is against me? Who has wronged us? And now,
the Great Mothers are here. They never grow old.
They circle the horizon. They're silvery white, then blood
red. They're dark and brazen, their cups never empty.
They'll never fail or fold.

Improvising: News We Carry

There is such beauty
in our runic flesh
Blossom dissolves darkness

Come out among
trees and wastelands
indecorous as poems

Hold my hand as we dance
new as rain

New as what we carry
in our pockets
like lost toys

Weather finds us draped
like leaves
curves of coming and going

To be with skin
held in tongues
of sunlight

The padlock drops away

How Alike Is Likeness?

I am like
you and do I like
you yes you yes who I like
are like
me in liking
what is not alike
in liking
so we wrap the liking
into shape and so we get to the truth of the liking
of me not being like
you but I like
you liking
me and we will live this likeness
as being liking
rather than alikened
to what you might like
or what I might like
as someone who likes
you and in that way a truth if you like
is like
you and I am like
you in this all truthfulness liking.

As If The Large Magellanic Cloud Looks Over Us

Thursday was full moon   more than silvery
when clouds parted   life is short   days are long
   you don't need me to tell you that   time is adjusted
to make it so   evening full of light   pink on gum trees
lorikeets gush out from the thick weave of branches

In the kitchen I bring together some simple vegetables
   it's not a dance   something emerges   they merge
the soup ladle is silvery   life is short

Uranus is three billion kilometres away
undetected until 13 March 1781   so far as we know

Some shorebirds will leave soon   Ruddy Turnstone
Red Knot, Sanderling   you have to drive an hour or so
to see them   someone tags them   then they go
along the East Asian-Australasian Flyway

I wonder if they smell the grape harvest   this summer
long and dry   that will make acidic whites rich shiraz
will bushfire smoke affect some pickings   I sip wine
before pouring the glass   into the pan
sugar and acid mean something   days are long

Something I've been reading reminds me
poems have centres that move   or is it borders
   I wish I'd made a note   I think they are islands
once parts of continents   their beaches
   submerged or lush

There are languages here I don't know   names
    Karrawirra Parri   Tarndanyangga   and I don't know
what birds say   the trees   possums   the bats
I hear them sometimes   in the thick weave

The day is playing its tricks   uncovering the sun
then covering it up   at night there've been clouds
like furry islands with lit-up seas   we wonder if
there's a possum landing on the roof some nights   or a cat

I don't remember   just what I was saying
to someone now dead   or lost in history   near borders

I wake from dreams   of profit and loss   in the warm breath
morning   a sound is running   a name I'm not sure of
    and here are my arms

Incarnations

The bee has died in the water
　　but that's not how everything dies
A breeze dies and is reborn
　　　as if it's continuous when it's a flutter
　　　　　like the sadness of blood in your chest
the uncanny offbeats like wings
Or a plane lands badly　　somewhere

The sun disappears but it's not dead
　　　though somehow it's a ghost of a larger plan
　　　　　that changes every time I stop
and gaze up at night　　although a cycle
　　　isn't simply a twist　　when I'm walking
　　　　　and a large discarded seed catches
under my foot so I trip
　　　but I know I was once inside
　　　　　a seed and another seed　　tiny footless
and waiting

How have the bees planned
　　to stop being so dead in the water
Is it sad to eat all this honey and not
　　　to think of its life and death as flowers
　　　　　drop and dry out　　like that bone you found
just under the topsoil the other day
　　　and that was a day that vanished like galaxies

The tree dangles down and I see butterflies flutter
    almost frantic along the nectar
Somehow I think this is the way
    I will vanish along a path gathering
        what I think I need or discarding seconds
and minutes   discarding heat by degrees
    like a sun or a blossom   but how does
        the plane cope with all that sky

I've never touched a cloud
Each time I look out the window
    they look cold even in summer
If a cloud could hold me up
    o how I would live

The Gap In The Trees

I'm less articulate than grass.
I hobble on my syllables
hoping something will surrender
a thought, maybe, a kindness,
a practicality.
A gap in the trees before sunset
does more.

The wind picks up
as the horizon I stare at
slips away from
the slope of today's sun.
In some places there are no days.
I could write it down
but who knows what colour
anything is?
Does the sun have a colour?
Does water?

I don't think birds do anything
in sentences
though I'm just making that up.
You don't need a philosopher
to know everything changes.
You can't step into a moment twice.
My thoughts waver
but not like a leaf.
It's a manner of speaking.

If I thought talking to the sun
would help, I would
but the gap in the trees darkens.
The grass becomes fainter.
Whatever darkness is
it's almost here. I turn on the light.
The light lights the room.
Nothing is inevitable.
Though maybe it is.

An Inexact Science

The air in the waiting rooms and corridors is talking
if you eavesdrop – but I'm not yet prepared.
If you listen to my bloodstream, you can hear it speak.
The heart's graph is difficult to decipher
but that's condition normal. And how I'll wake up later.
The medication becomes tomorrow's headache.
Someone calls my name. Someone else stands up.
I feel like going a-wandering as if I'm testing a theory.
My stockinged feet patter on the entire carpet.
I hope I don't lose my shoes.
I check myself with the nearest instrument.
My heart beats like a monitor, a probe, a drip.
Sometimes the body requires equipoise
and sometimes an alarm.

The clinical equipment is rolled back into the bin.
I want real love now.
Someone's looking for the Communications Book.
That seems to be the nub of it.
The forms are also part of the gymnastic.
Does anyone truly understand this unearthly language?
Something's been unfettered at the core.
Multiple choice is a game. But I'm quit with thread.
You can be sown up a million times and it still hurts.
Though it also sings – there is that.

I could sit down and loosen this opportunity.
I could unfold the printout. I could cry in the chapel.
I could lie down in the carpark and see what happens.
It's another theory. But can it stop now?
Can we throw open the excellent shutters
let in the various night?
In the west, buildings look like distant trees.
The once-remarkable shadows join together.
I could be one of them. I have a backpack
a phone, a folder. I can do anything.
I wear a blue gown.
Even the weather is blue, on the footpath,
in the branches, along the back alley.
Safety can be a kind of exclusion zone.
But it's an inexact science that gossip
almost prepares you for.
My name circles my arm, upside down,
smelling of plastic and disinfectant.
I am about to fold, as if it were a disguise.

Difficult Poem

(yeah, like a

lucid tiff   fit of plum   dolt cuff

epic mould   cute plod   dulcet mop

coiffed lump   polemic fit   demotic puff

muffled tic   code flip   deficit flop

melodic if   cleft podium   iced muff

tumid elf   difficult mope   lucid top

Mad Remedies

I try to avoid making anyone mad
as crazed boffins bathe me with advice
and sex cleansing.
Down comes my dress
soft to scientific trace.
Kama Sutra wax has a practical magic (with cinnamon flavour).

A mathematician asks 'why so much water'
as university tests expand my charisma
with ancient gender charts and hipster baths.
Female sex books celebrate my edgy detox
with full body disclaimer.
Bathe in horny response cream.

My joie de vivre is transmitted through
the only mysteries allowed:
arousal, nervousness
and sincere bath liquid.
Release sexual power of pheromones for only $24.99!!

I thoroughly buff my dirty thoughts
with vibrations and liquor.
I like nothing more than taking the waters
with elite and discerning candles.
I soap to remember!

Improvising Autumn

Geography includes inhabitants and vessels.
Gertrude Stein

How many passports do I need?

The sun comes and goes.

Is there a geography that explains me?

*

Are memories always green or simply improved
by weathering?

How young am I to be ancient with feelings
and lichen?

We hope the temperature lets our clothes dry, though
too many days here have been dry.

*

Are the maps complexes or excuses
from history?

Are geometries simply a way to triangulate sunshine, feeling,
and the return of the Eastern Spinebill to the yard?

My thoughts make sense of my tables and shelves, or
maybe it's the other way round.

*

Some days I think the bus stop resents me
and I keep waiting.

It's the end of daylight savings, the end of
something, a kind of autumn.

Are these mating pigeons simply flaunting
life, as they should?

*

But the birds have no passports.
Geography doesn't need me.

Memories may not exist.
I don't know what lichen might feel.

Maps are only warped perspectives.
Geometry's never easy in sunlight.

*

Chicken. Egg. Feather. Fall.

Or I walk out and stand in this air.

It's all I can know.

These Things (braided)

How   the city Was grey though it was Summer   and
everyone was thinking Christmas holidays
A siren runs past   the night And   it almost
enters me Like   an alarm already my body
Is   full of alarm Can   I hold your hand It   will
make me   less alarmed It   will make Me more
for   panic The   siren is no excuse What   if
someone is dying   they   treat You   tenderly but
firmly In   an   ambulance you feel so alive Like   a
body feels as   avenues Pass   you or you pass them I   am
easy to see Even   in cool   wintry Dark
Perhaps   I could be a beach Or   part of an ocean
Once   that would have seemed Swell   but now it's
dirty as   everything Perhaps   yes   that siren Perhaps   no

Or   a   meteor's tail That   streaked over the
city Last   Tuesday   like an alarm   I didn't see it Somebody
did   I usually miss These   things I daydream at
coagulating Full   of whistles Indirection bad chapters
Misquotes   infusions A   plastic hum I'm   not prepared
passing as a Human As   a woman As   a life form With   as
much skin They   attach a monitor I   Remember that
night And   read old stories of a coach That   arrives
for me   at last It   makes Little sound   the horses
However   are anxious they know It's   time for
me to go They   know it's time for   us all
They   know how   to see What   should be
alarmed Someone   will see us It   is Difficult to bear
the thought Of   being in the shape I'm in

The Dream Of The Real Thing

This dream was the most real thing I'd ever dreamed.
And it isn't a dream, it's still a childhood breath I'm hooked to,
its ether hefting through my mouth, down a real and unearthly
night river, while someone feels for a knife in the nearby world,
more illumined but no more terrible than this.

I am floating past murky widths, and why are there
owls here, so close, so sleepless, such birds, the hoo-hoo
of their wisdom, as if they knew looking down, eyes true-wide
upon my headway, how much a stranger I was and will be, heading
towards an eventual ocean.

I hear the yowl of some ancient animal. There it is!
Canine maybe, limp-footed, past its time, slinking away. Can I feel
sorry for its receding? In an eddy I notice some ragged thing floating
and circling, a crown of flowers and gold, but as I pass, I see
it's dull or counterfeit, plastic looped over wire.

The owls have dwindled, there's a rushing of rapids,
a whirlpool. I think this is when I must be overturned, when
I must be woken.

I just catch a smell, further foam where goddesses
are born, and monsters, the way home, maybe, the surge between
the great southern ocean and the north, the eastern sea and
the infinite west, a where that's not here.

I blink into brisk new light that looks fake
and ordinary, clinging to a metal stalk or branch. There was never
a flower stank so dull as this, no more proper uptight doom
than this chemical return.

In a bed, I'm a fresh routine creature, yet
behind my eyes I see the dream tide still, soundtracked by
the hey-ho of unmooring.

There are times I lose track of how many cells are mine or simply memory. Memory doesn't exist and it's always there, making you. Well, of course, I haven't kept track. Who could ever do that? But I know there is a trace, just as the morning knows you, not as a miracle nor as the ordinary, but the way things move.

There are times when I think about what it would be like to be a bird. And, yes, I am an animal, but a peculiar kind. I also wonder what it would be like to be a shadow, or grass.

Step Shadow

Early afternoon stretches along the street.
Honeyeaters cling onto wires.

My footsteps are buried in the pavement
like a prayer that never surfaces.

The light within light contracts and travels.
Half-remembered cadences roll over a fence.

The hour seems to drape.
Trees invent shadow.

A jet's underside pushes into the west.
Nearby, the shorebirds will soon fly north.

Concrete slowly flakes
as if it's also going somewhere.

Elegiac Continuum

As though I'd lived in some days that felt
right, but in others where I felt all the gas was gone,
our horoscopes crumpling like wacky movie sets
whose details were out-of-time in the bogus light.
As we passed the tremendous neon present
and its wanton sparkle, every toy
was us and smelled of pine air freshener.

I was writing again, to no-one, but diligently,
painfully, then out of the blue, I demounted
from the truck into a baffling, besotted twilight.
It spoke as I used to speak, a voice, defiant as
the crushed but beating world. Perhaps
it was chance, a ghost, the machine of the heart,
my bloody old nerve, still singing the continuum.

History

I am a history of product updates
a history of the grit in my shoes
of dirty currents, of piss and vinegar
of grapevines, of fake news

I am a history of stretched air
of shade, of dirty dirty coal
a history of monetisation
of hedge funds, sulfur clouds

I am a history of distant sunlight
a history of what I'm not
of eggs and baskets, apps and trolls
of dogs eating dogs

I am a history of what I deny
of wardrobe failure, organic polymers
a history of promises and rose gardens
of mists and fruitfulness, whatever is melting

I am a history of garden paths
a history of wild oats and thyme
of sinking islands, daisies and ashes
the rains down in Africa

I am a history of deep time and deep shit
a history of what was fat in the land
a history of very thin ice
a history of what I'll become

One City Is Another (alt space mix)

pluck each word
along my indolent sinew

this gown this shirt this glove
     it all may turn around

cadence drapes it adjusts
around that satin in the breeze
     in dreams
that meddle

even the embraces
I failed at in the room
paint them cover them

blushes
their needless opera

everything's a terrible plan
recordless trance

I wake up in fragments
one city   another

In Flight Entertainment

'no more blues', that's not a promise
there's no traction or policy in the blues

all those bars are too long a cycle
to make for twittering views

no more plaints or graces
no thanks, 'watch and listen carefully'

enhanced performance, premium economy
'a loss of consciousness', 'oxygen will flow', 'settle back'

it's a field day under the smoky hills

what does my tray table say about me
the colour of my life jacket, indeed, my life

'woke up this morning', that line's been used
an immense dark blue sea nothing like the Pacific

it's a long way down, it's a long way home
even the clouds are small

perhaps something scary or precious
will break loose as the screens fall

what if there were no more blues
everything white and cloudy, 'nothing to see here'

does Europe seem safe
there are checks again in the Schengen zone

'strong margins', more landings on Lesbos
ancient songs for peace, love, weddings, thanks

'persons of interest', abductions
the last Commodore rolls out of the factory

what do you do with your hands
time is pressing, 'enjoy the service'

showers in Cape Town, sunny and dry in Lima

your own youtube channel must be full of likes as well as gripes
as the news disappears into itself, by jings it's hard

but not so hard as no more blues

and there's New South Wales or whatever it was
or will become, cultivated white squares and a haze

'being a personal trainer', 'a true Aussie lifestyle'
from Port Macquarie to Wagga Wagga

which state would you settle in
'the Australian dream ticks all the boxes'

no more blues, it's all white from now on
'a loss of consciousness', 'settle back' –

Murray Andante

The night fills with Bach
with the clear cold
a gas fire doesn't touch
outside rattle of a skateboard
not gelling with the violin

skateboard guy, I've seen him before
rolls back towards Gilbert Street
the slow movement begins
it's not quite a baroque town
the grids almost classical

but the Bach andante claims it
now the outside softens
again giving access somehow
to measure, of steady streets
lack of blue shadow and a

width of days along with my
steady lostness in a bowl
of clarity, while above my eyes
the green and grey hills
need to stretch my thought

and rain suddenly hits the roof
then stops, quick, all this water
that doesn't go to rivers
that doesn't cease the drought
nor bring me back to

a mind that accompanied me
once through punky allegros
and andantes and other
more humid songs
unlike the passing of trams at

Pirie Street, as lawyers progress
to sandstone courts where
cameras linger, sensations of the local
a city's petty crimes
well, that's cross continental

like the sad river, as even
the blind hours remind me
killed state by state, classical neglect
not even this rain nor
this music allays.

Not A Theory Of Origins

I don't know the real names
of things here, I never will –
the berries, bugs, birds, rustling noises,
foodstuffs, bricks, bottlebrush, eaves –
they were named before we came here,
in the kit of histories, recurrences
of older sung stories, their sound
their families, human and nonhuman,
unfolding.

I walk among it collecting
used tickets, leaves, compost and string
for garbage night, folding fragile sheets,
laying out forks, rice and vegetables,
whatever resounds in my hand,
a wine glass decades old, last of a set
– and two years ago he died, and
I hadn't seen him for years.

I can never say I'm nowhere.
We're always passing time and shadows
in some hallway between
plaster and dust, or welcoming
the quick of all these green and yellow
apertures, daylight cracks.

The sun was still warm today
though autumn's fading the air
and my heaviness shades into the yard

with its grit memory of bacteria
and spore, while birds settle
into evening, as always blackbirds
scatter the ground, a wagtail flutters
between rooflines, lorikeets quarrel
in the dimming.

Tonight starry origins rain down
on us as they always do.
I don't know what birds call home.
We've no territory like an old country,
but we talk through days gone
and foreseen, imagined necessities,
those fantastic ideals, where old friends
have left, all the while coaxing
a sweet temporary quietness.
The sky isn't a home. Today
it was impossibly blue.

With Blue And Yellow Wings

The temperature around the house is unsteady
and the Prime Minister can't seem to talk level about anything.

There's tenderness under my eye where bones are weary
and now here's breakfast and the beginning of division.

Each tablet has its reason.

Gold deposits have been found in mulga leaves, yes, we're
        always seeking
the motherlode, but I sniff the wind and the melting ice.

Reading this article about the history of Gay Liberation
        got me thinking
how we learned to hide things. Listen, my left ear seems to contain
        a pulsing sea.

For days there's been blood at the back of my throat.

I miss the roses and their blowsy cheeks and, while I think of it
my father's painting has been with me a long time.

Fitful rain makes its shifty jazz on the paving, as every day curls
round itself in airy gaiety and the wash of time.

The train horn is arousing.

But hey, just outside it was, just outside, the large parrot
with blue and yellow wings on the bottlebrush, on the magnolia,
        just outside.

Clouds absorb the lateness of the day, the once-exceptional shadows
join together, a calmative, a serene and deliberate notion.

Everything sings if you listen hard.

The Light Of The Plants That Are Growing

(a cento)

I am a reed. My river waits reply.
An old shell singing.
I never yield but wait.

Across the red sky two birds flying.
Little voices of the air. A ribbon at a time.
Ways one could be learning to use in being gay.

I whirl like leaves in roaring wind.
The blood is listening in my frame.
The skirt. And water.

You mean ocean water.
Not exactly an ocean a sea. A success.
The tawny sweetwinged thing.

Yes we see it every night near the hills.
This is so natural. Birds do it.
We do not know their name.

I held her hand the tighter.
Shadows hold their breath.
With what. With what I said.

Improvising: Of Sheer Now

Everything ancient is
among flights
of sheer now
Even my hair is singing

I fall over days
vaster than history
I can't put the leaves back

The dark is fresh
as rot, just the way
a room is
queer within

Lick plethora
the crushed rose inside me

Recompose me
in my profane air
my homely head

Touches / Touches Us

Everything Touches

If there is light   there
must be dark   if in   the dark
   you wait a   while   un
til   a different   moon re
turns there's no   proper   distance

after Mark Rothko, *1957 #20*

RootSky

darklight   darkdog sleeps
a tree grows   in the heart we're
   cloudmud children   you
give me plant   fire   I'm a cre
vasse   blood   flowers   milkdrop   earth

after Frida Kahlo, *The love embrace of the universe,
the Earth (Mexico), myself, Diego, and Señor Xólotl*

Your Eyelashes Like Grass

our pores   bloom   like roses
I sweep   dust out the   door its
   threads   blushes   tiny
flora   an interstellar
wind   carves nebulas   like grass

after Jackson Pollock, *Autumn Rhythm*

'Everything should be blue. But is it?'

what fell   from weather
o fabulous   mutinous
   machine   bending blue
waves   islands   flaking off   sky
stacks   skerries   makeshifts   singing

after Wilhelmina Barns-Graham,
Variations on a Theme – Splintered Ice No. 2

To go home   to the old home

to make   of spittle
and milk   to spill   as all   pig
ment   blood to   the fire
utterance   'oh'   uterus
nipple   tree   dirt   leaf   black moon

after Paul Klee, *Wald-Hexen (Forest Witches)*

~~what doesn't~~ **Touch us**   ~~hovers all~~ **The same**

waves   skulls   skin   seaweed
a flotilla   tangled lines
even   the invis
ible has   sound   oars drag   storm
ferocious   hours   tide loves

after Cy Twombly, *Lepanto Part III*

A Fantasia Of Oddments, Wagers And Zeroes

In the midst of afternoon   an unexpected hubbub above
parrots midair chasing a falcon   sun in my eyes I brush
light   the radiant-shaking leaves loosed from their crib
my first time free of blame for my ill-feeling   my dank
self-pity as a citizen of pain   sun's mocking me, its empire
large, ancient   while I cope with presence, motes, a fantasia
of being   even as small as the life forms on my skin greater
than earth's population   do they feel guilty like their host
or are they me   mostly empty, waiting for batteries, innards
sounding a sonorous plaint   I bless every idea, glance and jot
in my creases   as starlight feels its way, seems ever so keen
as I step forward slowly   shading my eyes from the luxury
the day's slough taste, plant oil, insect   joy of the meld
lifedeathlife nectar   planets as gods above it all, the nuzzle
of eternity terrors   while I'm heaving my ribs and oddments
looking for nightcusp   wineblood's less to blame, let it pour
with the backyard gladness, the universe honey   the quick
and freight of littlebig world, its evildoing   or pitiless raddle
of my circulation, CO_2 emissions, the west's bountiful sophistry
the wasteland of antibiotics, water features, and trolls
oh wait, honeyeaters hustle and drop   and I'm so ugh
wondering when all the oil will be gone   leaving vitriol
or a spangled release, an unguessed drug   or a wager
as if this is my portion I grab at the door   nothing x-ray
could determine   my mind's not a printout, it's a yammer
of lyric passionate as a forest   lost songs, the zeroes

How To Arrange The Mind:
Or What Is It You Love?

1. To open up the top of your head could be dangerous. If you do it at home, do it with a friend.

2. But can we ever get a handle on the brain? The brain is curly. So, maybe the mind is also a swirl.

3. Begin thinking! No, keep thinking.

4. There is no pause button.

5. Can you draw a picture of yourself? Or try drawing a picture of yourself drawing a picture of yourself.

6. Are you tired yet?

7. I wonder how much tiny time there is in a thought.

8. Stop thinking about thinking!

9. Yes, I'm getting tired. I'm getting thirsty.

10. Water isn't pure nor is wine. Some teas make the hands jittery.

11. Can you be in two spaces at once?

12. Shall I draw the first circle? I can make it a zero, a space, a loop, a hole.

13. Draw circles around my eyes. Draw a circle on my forehead. Draw circles on my tongue.

14. It takes time to draw, and where has that time taken me?

15. Time moves, not the clock. But clocks move inside themselves.

16. Time is relative. In relation to...who do you think?

17. Sappho says: What you love, is what is best.

18. Stay the night. We can slow the night down.

19. I don't know what you're thinking but you are here.

20. 'All night long' as the insomnia of love the poets write about.

21. Not all poets write about love.

22. Tonight, we're not reading those ones.

23. Tonight we thank the hands we have. In that way we can begin.

24. The brain's too big to handle. I've been thinking about this a lot. But the average brain only weighs 1.35 kilos. Three pounds in the old system.

25. A brain is worth more than that, surely.

26. The brain is too big to handle.

27. Touch the top of my head. (You do it thoughtfully.)

28. In the sky above our heads, the divine numbers are a gamble.

29. Zero is a place to begin. A circle. A number without number.

30. We're not one. We're not many. We're all that, here. I think that's plenty and enough.

Serious Wavering

within this dotty sunlight
and gusts of beams on a wall
shadows sway in
queer bevelled *trémulo*
make abstract shape
on ground's blebs and gash tricks

as light without maps
like cosmos winks
like ribbons and motes
inventories to exploit
as mossy tokens wrinkle
a bower with its prism

Unguided Meditation

Tolerate the spasmodic, the obscure, the fragmentary, the failure.
Virginia Woolf, 'Mr Bennett and Mrs Brown'

i.
I am hanging onto the edge of a continent.
The full moon takes the sand far from the beach
    into the gulf's indifference.
I stand for a moment in this immodest heat.
The world here will burn before it freezes.
The words I write, and the sun, all resist me.
So they should.

ii.
As a child I'd pad around thinking 'if I were a boy',
another kind of mind and muscle, a difference
as green as grass but it never worked. TV was
my co-parent, my super hero. The outside air filled
with mowers. Nothing would fit the cracks.
Every bird was a visitor, while I stumbled into bricks
or the hidden kicks of the real world. That's how I fell.
    And how I felt. Each stitch was a prick.

iii.
Like Osiris or Frankenstein, I am assembled.

iv.
Later, when they poked out my eye and stuck in
another, they forgot to tell me it wouldn't fit quite right,
or I'd be able to see far, predict every calamity,
but everyone would laugh.
    (OK, have it your way.)
Each night I sit down and watch it watching me.

v.
Are poems becoming hotter and darker like the world?
Maybe I'm listening for the wrong broadcast
as a loner within screenlight, a bit '404 not found',
living in idle twilight among pickings of lecherous
sparrows, still subject of thanatos, still
hanging around my old address.
     Not all the boxes can be ticked.

vi.
The sea is my mother tongue, reaching for me
on the sand, my feet slipping in the undertow.
The tide wants me, my paper sails. Μὴ κίνη χέραδασ,
Sappho says. 'Don't stir up the beach rubble.'
     My fragments float.
Μνάσεσθαί τινά φαμι καὶ ὕστερον ἀμμέων.

Who has met their trash and forgiven it?
'One day someone   will remember us.'

The Coat That Doesn't Fit

Here on the once affluent lawn I'm surrounded
with boxes. I look into them, searching
for ghosts. They're now limp old shirts.
I've smelt smoke all morning, out of the south.

Here's the coat that still doesn't fit.
I empty the pockets. Look, a white glove
stained with blood, an angel's feather, a toy gun
with a broken trigger, a dry leaf.
Flames part the horizon.

A house is an ocean, once crammed with things,
caps, scrapbooks, isotopes, car bellies,
plastic twigs, corrupted memory. I grab
the coat that doesn't fit. I hide inside its arms.

Some things are finished. There are bones
that remain, bones that are dust.
I look at the feather, I look at the leaf.
They're almost the same shape.
A ship in the gulf is waiting for me.

What Sleep Is This?

What remains of us at night
The weight of respiration
   the insects we swallow
the division of thought into
   chemical haze

Far off there are holdfasts
lee shores, maybe an anchor
   or a compass
Leaves disturb the concrete
   while my eyelashes quiver

What memory might be dug up
by wind or an earth tremor
   a lost goodbye on a path
as clouds move
   in and out of the suburb

A breeze fumbles over
old cottages
   and mansions
There's a band of stars
   aching above the backyard

A succession of vehicles
roars away or comes too close
   I don't know if this is
a night dream
   or a morning dream

Some nights collude with
the galaxy's old glow
    They can be remote
as indifference
    or have metal and darkness

Spells For Futures

Fend off cloudy fashion

      Find more furrows and fill them

Undo blouses more often

      Ugh with care

Trace a word across the sheets

      Twist again, be a plant

Ululate freshly each day

      Undulate as well

Rescue leaves

      Run from the gate

Escape like a friend

      Enter every minute

Do, Make, Steal, Sing

Waver on stilts while listening to arias.

Sew your own rose and ask of its questions.

Steal flotsam like wanton flies.

Ruin lyrics, while above the egrets lift.

Paste green language around a cork room.

Refuse to 'nail it'. Just refuse.

Keep rearranging what is footnote and what is space.

Walk out one day in presences.

Take night's immediate nerve with possibility.

Speculate outside with the big southerly.

Pass as you go into.

Sleep all around at blue windows.

Burn down the villa, change all the doors.

Stand so shadows make you perfect.

Love your dumb corpus, of song.

A Week Is A Night In A Dream Of Sea, Stones & Trees

I kindle sleep   from halfwake breath | day's gall
I drink dusk into my self-house   swim past
    mad-sweet phone-texting stare
I jaywalk into night oceans   with memory swells

I turn my eye on how I fall   feel late light's vat pour
    weirder than street gleaning
head dream | heart dream   beyond car horn & blare
or my daily word switch   craft without craft

What is   the 'best of dreams'?
[When is my blood   on the right side of night?]

I am west-walking   quickened in moon-plane
at the arse-end of   any-day's crap & lather
I become part   of the spirit-gate
I take my own hand   No! Who takes my hand?
Who is dream-friend   not a pisstake?

Who begins to keen   turns on the live-stream
    other-world blether?
Who has formed this circle   I turn through?
Night-plough | knot-mover | REM-rem-rem

Or a soft hammer   in a yard I'm approaching
I grab this   push-pull door
for the long hall of the unreal   the long haul into night

Seeming I came here   through trouble dreams | all meet here
To come here to become   to become here to shatter

[Here is all the world   here is all another world
here is this&that | all together now | jumpcut | song jam]

I feed shiny poison to waves   sick meat to sharks
In sea fathoms some old thing sleeps   some older thing wakes
I see the eye of crusted deep-deeps   & the maw of what's broken
The ancient trees of seas   dead kelp | dead coral

Or I climb narrow steps   I slip on footings
I stumble slow stones   I am clinger | am crawler
I have come here with some tools   a bell | a rule
    a pen | a hammer | nails & tongs
to record   to recall | become here to shatter

Each tread its letter   I almost slip on the last step
I drop   all I have for making | tool   by tool   by tool
Each step its letter   the trees call out

H   huon pine
E   eucalypt
L   lemon
P   plum

U   ulmus
S   silky oak

On the empty branch-house   only three fruit remain
Below is a vine   as if the very heart of mayhem
as unrest within a breeze   on the starry leaves

In the way waves speak   do doors speak?
The wooden ones   holding the echo | each bad tongue makes
Which tree do I resemble   with my blag-face thought
in this land of opposite feet   this land of stake-flip | gut wrath
land grab | a shitload of sundering | official murder

The best of wood   is absent & gone
the long hall full of   turning-away sleep
the wood-wall is   no wonder now
Outside the bush waits its while | or cannot
Even the weeds | migrants | leafplush invaders | do say

W   wollemi pine
A   acacia
I   ironbark
T   tallowwood
?

O   olive
H   hop bush

N   nutmeg
O   orange
T   ti tree
!

Of What I'll Become

So some may say   everything falls
cities & repute   summer apricots
a small white plate
   rain on the gulf

The rough is more   than smooth
light is no more fleet   than time
   in fact –

Some say   this glass on the shore
is sharp   or smooth
rough as   broken stone   holds light
   as it holds time

Some say   that tide
is running   out then
   back upon us

But who are we   as
plastic beings
shells   shaped around   ventricles
& nodes   blood   polymer
   simple fear –

Among this winter kelp   these shadows
on the sand   pressed by futures
   & storms

Notes

Front epitaph: Quote in English from Sappho Fr.152 is my version of the Ancient Greek text.

'Where Do You Look?': refers indirectly to photographs in an exhibition, 'Diane Arbus: American Portraits', containing work by Dianne Arbus, Lisette Model, Mary Ellen Mark, Katy Grannan, William Eggleston, Weegee, Garry Winogrand and others at the Art Gallery of South Australia, 2018.

'Walking Home in the Dark Through a Succession of Categories': written after reading poems (in translation) by Helga Olshvang and Alla Gorbunova. In particular, a few words words from Olshvang's 'Can't We See Where We Are…' and Gorbunova's 'cities: an inventory' have been specifically reworked into similar phrasings, though entirely different contexts, in this poem.

'This Path is Our Season Tonight': uses a structure influenced by poems by Philip Nikolayev in his book *Monkey Time* and others of his works.

'Cursing Girl Gust': *heofon* is Old English for 'the sky' or 'heaven'.

'Consummations': consists of the three section break poems from a previous book of mine, *Brink*, Five Islands Press, 2017.

'The Morning, Not the Movie': 'schooey of New', in NSW, schooey is a shortened form of schooner, a measure of a glass of beer equalling 425 ml. New refers to Tooheys New, a common lager-style beer available in NSW, made famous in the 1970s through the advertising jingle 'I feel like a Tooheys…'.

'this make-believe this driftwood': Every word and/or phrase in this poem occurs across various poems in my first book, *The Mask and the Jagged Star*, Hazard Press, 1992.

'As Long as You Need/Fragments': the poem is a series of mistranslations, misunderstandings, or loose versions of several fragments from Sappho (in order following, mostly, the number system for the original Greek texts in the Lobel-Page edition, *Poetarum Lesbioram fragmenta*): Fr. 153, 130, 145, 36, 126, 104, 55, 44, 24, 30, 51, 105, 137, 147, 145, 58, 111, 52, 44, 2, 45.

'Far As the Night': The first line of the poem, from which the title is also derived, is a quote from Hélène Cixous's book, *Three Steps on the Ladder of Writing*.

'The Lost Child': in the last section, 'Fate', there is a reference to lines in the only surviving intact poem by Sappho, 'Hymn to Aphrodite'.

'As If The Large Magellanic Cloud Looks Over Us': In the Kaurna language, Karrawirra Parri refers to what white settlers called the River Torrens. Tarndanyangga is the Kaurna word for 'red kangaroo rock' and was used by the Kaurna people to refer to what is now the Adelaide city area. It also is the Kaurna name for Victoria Square in the Adelaide CBD.

'The Light of the Plants that are Growing': is a cento consisting solely of phrases/lines from poems by Emily Dickinson, Nos. 14, 72, 162, 320; Katherine Mansfield, 'Now I am a Plant, a Weed', 'Across the Red Sky', 'Voices of the Air'; H.D., 'She Contrasts With Herself Hippolyta'; Gertrude Stein, 'Lifting Belly', as well as versions of Sappho by Percy Bysshe Shelley, 'To Constantia, Singing'; Alfred Tennyson, 'Fatima'; Algernon Swinburne, 'Songs of the Springtides'; and Elizabeth Barrett Browning, 'Song of the Rose', words from this last forming the poem's title.

'How To Arrange the Mind: Or What Is It You Love?': In stanza no. 17, the reference to Sappho is to Fr. 16. In no. 20, the reference to 'all night long' is to Sappho, Fr. 41, as well as a personal recollection of the Lionel Richie song, 'All Night Long', playing during a past Sydney Gay and Lesbian Mardi Gras Parade.

'Unguided Meditation': versions of lines and phrases from Sappho are my own. The poem's last line 'translates' the phrase in Ancient Greek that is the last line of the previous stanza.

'A Week Is A Night In A Dream Of Sea, Stones & Trees': incorporates reconfigurations of a few phrases and ideas from 'The Dream of the Rood' and 'Beowulf' as well as a gesture towards the arboreal names of the letters in the Scots-Irish Gaelic alphabet (my thanks to Kirsten Norrie (MacGillivray) for suggesting this approach).

'Of What I'll Become': the repeated phrase 'some say' echoes Sappho Fr. 16.

Acknowledgements

A number of the poems in this book were first published in various print or online periodicals and anthologies, some in different forms or versions and/ or with different titles. I would like to thank the editors of the following:

4W, ars poetica (USA), *The Australian, Australian Poetry Journal, Back Story, Bent Street, Burning House Press* (UK), *The Canberra Times, Cordite Poetry Review, datableedzine* (UK), *The Disappearing: Red Room Poetry, foam:e, Golfo, The Griffith Review, Hecate, Island, Jacket2* (USA), *Mascara Literary Review, Meanjin, Meniscus, Modern Poetry in Translation* (UK), *Not Very Quiet, Otoliths, Overland, Plumwood Mountain, Transnational Literature, Vlak* (Czech Republic), *Westerly, Wet Ink*

'Filthy Distance', as an untitled poem, first appeared in the chapbook *Senses Working Out*, Vagabond Press, 2012.

'All That Shudder' first appeared in *Shuffle: An anthology of micro lit*, ed. Cassandra Atherton, Spineless Wonders Press, 2019.

'In Flight Entertainment' also appeared in *The Best Australian Poems 2016*, ed. Sarah Holland-Batt, Black Inc, 2016.

'Murray Andante' also appeared in *The Best Australian Poems 2017*, ed. Sarah Holland-Batt, Black Inc, 2017.

'Do Make Steal Sing' (as 'Things to Make and Do') also appeared in *poem, home: An Anthology of Ars Poetica*, eds Jennifer Hill and Dan Waber, Paper Kite Press, Kingston PA, 2009.

The short works situated in the midst of each section of this book under the collective title of 'Improvising' were published as a single poem, 'Improvisings. Of Sheer Now', in *Cordite Poetry Journal*, Issue 93, Nov 2019.

My thanks to Camille Roulière for alerting me to the words of Alphonse de Lamartine and Antoine-Laurent de Lavoisier. Special thanks to Terri-ann White for being open to this version of an earlier manuscript, for good advice, as well as her ongoing support for Australian poetry through UWA Publishing.

As always, and above all, my love and thanks to Annette Willis, for ideas, understanding and, most importantly, constant love.